OIL AND WATER
A Look at the Middle East

by Glen Swanson
illustrations by Jill Shaffer

Prentice-Hall, Inc.
Englewood Cliffs, New Jersey

Printed in the United States of America   ·J
Prentice-Hall International, Inc., London
Prentice-Hall of Australia, Pty. Ltd., North Sydney
Prentice-Hall of Canada, Ltd., Toronto
Prentice-Hall of India Private Ltd., New Delhi
Prentice-Hall of Japan, Inc., Tokyo
Prentice-Hall of Southeast Asia Pte. Ltd., Singapore
Whitehall Books Limited, Wellington, New Zealand

10 9 8 7 6 5 4 3 2 1

LIBRARY OF CONGRESS CATALOGING IN PUBLICATION DATA
Swanson, Glen.   Oil and water.
SUMMARY: Explores the historic and current importance
of oil and water in countries of the Middle East.
1. Petroleum—Near East—Juvenile literature.
2. Water-supply—Near East—Juvenile literature.
1. Petroleum—Near East. 2. Water supply—Near East
I. Title.
80-27746   TN870.3.S95   333.91'00956
ISBN 0-13-633677-9

Contents

For my daughters, Heidi and Kristine

The author wishes to express his thanks to the following organizations for technical information concerning oil and water: Arabian American Oil Company (Aramco), *Aramco World, Aramco and Its World,* company handbooks and annual reports; American Petroleum Institute, *Facts About Oil;* Chevron, U.S.A., Inc., *The Story of Oil;* Exxon Corporation, *Middle East Oil,* and *The Lamp;* Mobil Oil Corporation, *Mobil World, Mobil Overview, The Language of Oil;* Texaco Inc., *The Texaco Star;* American Water Works Association; United States Department of Interior and Department of State; National Academy of Sciences, *More Water for Arid Lands: Promising Technologies and Research Opportunities ;* Shell Oil Company, *The Story of Petroleum.*

He also wishes to express his appreciation to Joan Butler and Faith Hanson, who introduced him to the enjoyment of writing for young people, and to his wife, Annagreta, for her warm encouragement and helpful criticism.

Oil and Water

Oil and water. The future of our world depends upon these two liquids.

Water is our most precious resource. Without it, there would be no life on earth.

Oil does not support life as water does, yet it is also precious. Our modern way of living depends on oil. It provides energy for our homes and schools, for our cities and industries, for our airplanes and cars.

There is enough oil and enough water available now to support us for a few more years. But some people have too much oil and not enough water, while others have enough water but not enough oil. The balance between the supplies of these two valuable liquids and the needs for them throughout the world is a problem of crucial importance.

Nowhere are oil and water more important than in the Middle East. It has been estimated that the region contains over half of the world's crude oil reserves. The United States and other industrialized nations depend upon oil from the Middle East to meet their increasing energy demands. The Middle East is responding to the world's requirements and is shipping millions of barrels daily to distant destinations. But as it responds, the Middle East must also consider its own situation and its own needs, especially its need for water.

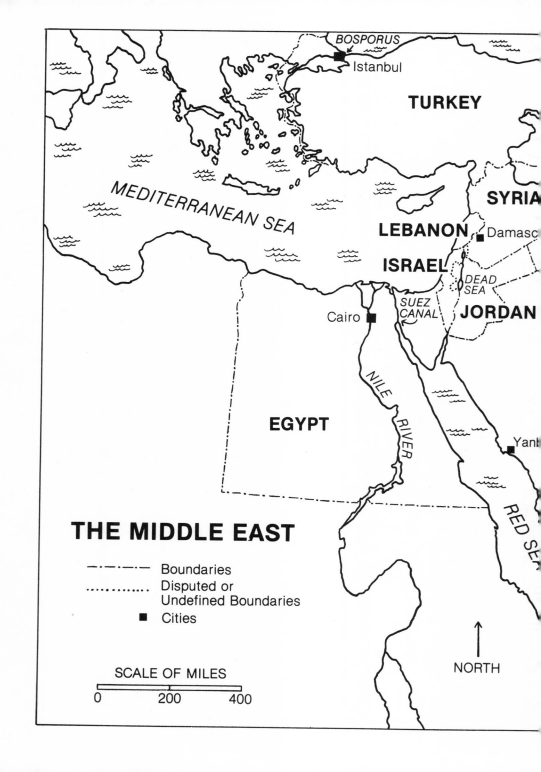

BOSPORUS

Istanbul

TURKEY

MEDITERRANEAN SEA

SYRIA

LEBANON

Damasc

ISRAEL

DEAD
SEA

SUEZ
CANAL

JORDAN

Cairo

NILE RIVER

EGYPT

Yan

RED SE

THE MIDDLE EAST

—·—·—· Boundaries
·············· Disputed or
Undefined Boundaries
■ Cities

SCALE OF MILES

0   200   400

NORTH

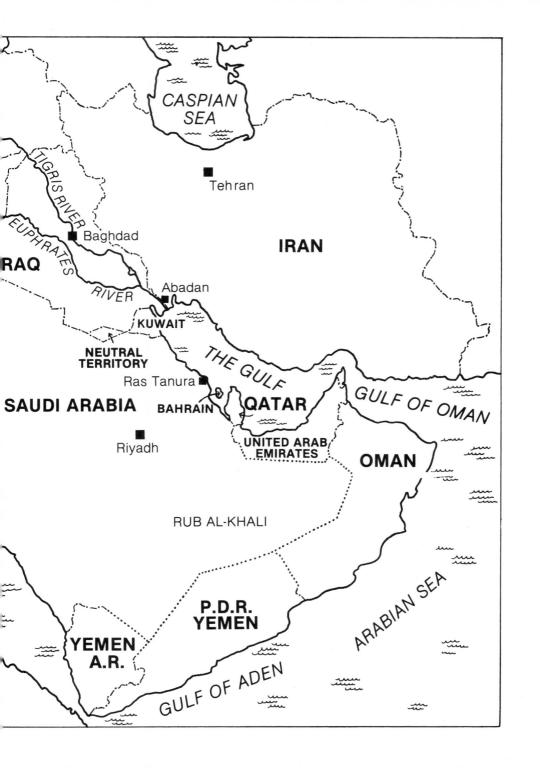

Water in the Middle East

Water has been, and is still, the bloodstream of Middle Eastern civilization. Some of the world's greatest rivers are here, such as the Nile, the Tigris, and the Euphrates. Ancient civilizations clung to the banks of these life-giving waterways and grew into strong empires. For thousands of years, Egypt on the Nile and Mesopotamia on the Tigris and Euphrates were rivals for power. Their economies were based on elaborate systems of artificial irrigation, using the waters of the great rivers.

THE NILE

Life in ancient Egypt was governed by the Nile. The Nile was predictable. It overflowed its banks so regularly that a calendar was based on its rhythm. It carried rich silt down from the mountains and deposited it on the flat land each year when it overflowed. This provided excellent soil for growing crops. A strong central government led by rulers called pharaohs made certain that the Nile's precious waters were used efficiently. Protected by the mighty pharaohs, the Egyptians grew the finest wheat in the ancient world. The men who owned the wheat gained riches and power from the fertile land created by the river. As the fifth-century Greek historian Herodotus remarked, Egypt is the "Gift of the Nile."

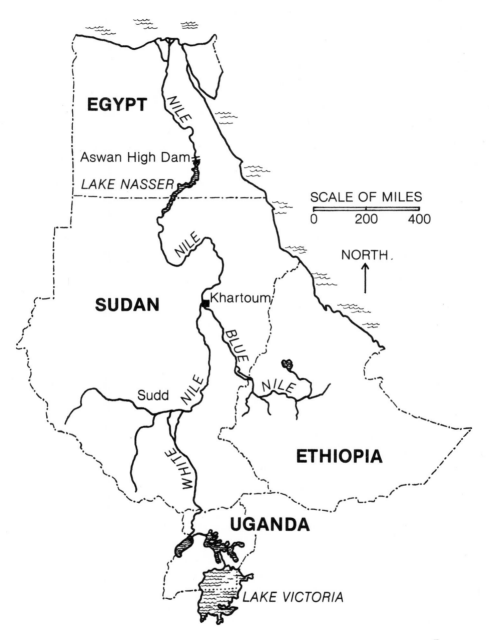

EGYPT

NILE

Aswan High Dam

LAKE NASSER

NILE

SCALE OF MILES

0   200   400

NORTH.

SUDAN

Khartoum

BLUE

NILE

Sudd

NILE

WHITE

ETHIOPIA

UGANDA

LAKE VICTORIA

5

Many people think of the Nile River as entirely Egyptian. But this is not so. One major branch of the river, the White Nile, arises on the Equator in Uganda's Lake Victoria. To reach Egypt, the White Nile has to pass through the Sudd, located in the southern half of the Sudan. The Sudd is an immense swamp, the size of Florida, where much water is lost through seepage and evaporation. Even with this loss, the White Nile pushes northward, supplying a steady flow of water throughout the year. At Khartoum it is joined by the other major branch, the Blue Nile. The Blue Nile begins in the highlands of Ethiopia. It carries the torrential rains of summer through the Sudan to Egypt. Because of this combination of lake and mountain-rain water sources, the Nile can supply water to Egypt and the Mediterranean Sea not only in winter, when the need is less, but also in summer when the need is greater.

Modern times have brought change to the Nile River valley in Egypt. In the 1960's the Aswan High Dam was completed. It controls the flood water, releasing it into irrigation canals as it is needed.

Under the old system, flood waters were collected in basins for irrigation. The basins have been replaced by a network of canals and ditches that provide irrigation for two or three growing seasons per year. As in past generations, these irrigation requirements dominate the daily activity of many Egyptians. Mechanical water pumps do assist irrigation, but many farmers still water their fields in the traditional ways, raising the river water with a bucket on a water lift and using draft animals to power water wheels.

The more modern ways of water control have opened new land to irrigation; they have also brought problems. As water flows through the ground, it dissolves minerals from the soil. Water that contains salt or dissolved minerals is called saline water. As the saline water evaporates, the dissolved minerals or salts are left on the soil. This buildup of salt deposit is harmful to the soil, making it less fertile for crops. In Egypt, the old method of irrigation brought rich silt down from the highlands along with the water. This meant new soil was added each year, and the fields did not become too salty. But the new methods of irrigation hold back the silt, allowing salts to build up in the old soil.

Waterlogging is also a problem. Because the Nile is so large and seemingly everlasting, water is wasted in the countryside. Farmers tend to open the irrigation sluices and let too much water flow into the fields. If you stick your finger into such waterlogged ground, water seeps out. Much cultivated land has been ruined by waterlogging. One method to correct this problem has been to install underground drain pipes to lead off the surplus water.

Since Egypt shares the Nile with other countries, international political problems may arise. For example, if the Sudan draws off water or if Ethiopia builds its own dams and irrigation systems on the Blue Nile, the water supply bound for Egypt will be reduced. This political issue is not unique to the Nile River countries. Similar problems in the use and control of water and waterways can be found in many other places, such as the border region between Iraq and Iran.

THE RIVERS OF IRAQ

In ancient times, Iraq had an effective irrigation system based on the Euphrates and Tigris rivers. Cities and empires flourished on these waterways. But over the centuries, the irrigation works were destroyed in warfare or suffered from neglect. During the twentieth century much work has been done to improve the irrigation systems, to build new dams, to develop better use of available water resources.

Except for the rainy areas of northeastern Iraq, most of the country has too little rainfall for agriculture and continues to rely primarily on the Tigris and Euphrates. Both rivers originate in the mountains of eastern Turkey; they join in Iraq about 100 miles from the head of the Gulf, (which is known to Iranians as the Persian Gulf and to Arabs as the Arabian Gulf). There they form the Shatt-al-Arab River, which then flows to the Gulf. The most important settled and cultivated areas of Iraq are the lands along the banks of the Tigris and Euphrates. But here, too, the fertile land has suffered from the problem of salinity—the accumulation of mineral salts in the soil.

The Shatt-al-Arab is also the name for the region surrounding the Shatt-al-Arab River. Part of this region forms the boundary between Iran and Iraq. Tension over the question of water rights and navigation has, at times, led to fighting. The region and river are made even more important by the presence of the key oil refinery at Abadan.

UNDERGROUND WATER IN IRAN

In Iran, the large rivers are not as dependable as the Nile is in Egypt. Maximum rainfall occurs during the winter months or early spring. The amount of rainfall varies greatly from year to year. At certain times of the year the rivers swell with rushing water, which is contained by dams until needed. But this surge of water lasts only for a few weeks. Then, for a while, there is barely a trickle of water. And if the rains fail, the rivers dry up. Because the rivers are not dependable, water must be found in some other way.

Thousands of years ago, the people of Persia (the former name for Iran) irrigated the land by digging a system of underground water channels called *qanats*. Many of these qanats are still used today. They are based on water located

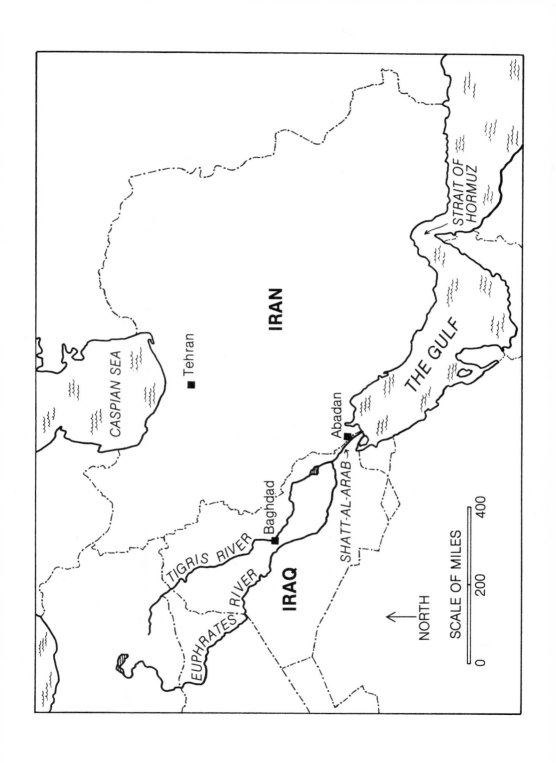

inside a hill or mountain. To tap this underground water, a well shaft is sunk in the hillside down to the water table (the level of the underground water). Horizontal galleries ray out from the bottom of the shaft to catch the water from the basin or table. At the bottom of the slope, near the village where the water is to be used, a trench is dug. The trench enters the earth and becomes a tunnel aimed slightly upward toward the water table inside the mountain. When this sloping horizontal tunnel connects with the vertical master well shaft, the whole system can lead the water outside to the lower point where the trench begins. Between the well shaft (or head well) and the exit, a series of vertical shafts are opened for ventilation and removal of debris.

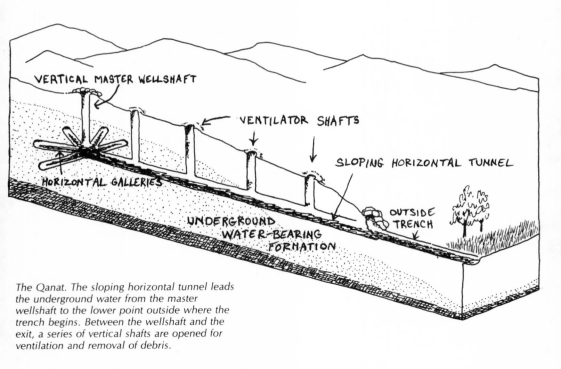

VERTICAL MASTER WELLSHAFT

VENTILATOR SHAFTS

SLOPING HORIZONTAL TUNNEL

HORIZONTAL GALLERIES

UNDERGROUND WATER-BEARING FORMATION

OUTSIDE TRENCH

The Qanat. The sloping horizontal tunnel leads the underground water from the master wellshaft to the lower point outside where the trench begins. Between the wellshaft and the exit, a series of vertical shafts are opened for ventilation and removal of debris.

Because qanats need no pumps to deliver water, they can be used where pumped wells are too costly to operate. Farmers in Iran are still using old qanats, some as much as 40 miles long, to bring underground water to the dry plains. But few new ones are being built. Even with modern machinery, it is costly to keep the tunnels free of dirt. In addition, qanats are dangerous to build, because the underground structure can give way during construction and trap the worker in a mud or rock slide.

OTHER MIDDLE EASTERN WATER RESOURCES

One of the surprises in the Middle East is the Caspian Sea area. Because so much rain falls on the land near this sea, there are jungles like those in the tropics. The Caspian Sea lies between the Soviet Union and Iran, and it is the largest landlocked body of fresh water in the world. Every year it grows smaller. If the rivers of Iran emptied into it, the Caspian Sea would be huge. But because of the way the mountains formed, the rivers and streams flow not into the Caspian but into the inland deserts where they eventually disappear.

Between Egypt and the plateau countries of Turkey and Iran lie several Middle Eastern countries with extraordinary water regions. In Jordan there is a huge gash in the earth's surface called the Great or Jordan Rift, through which the Jordan River passes. The Rift is deepest in the Jordan Valley and the Dead Sea. From its source near the Lebanese border, the Jordan River twists southward to the Dead Sea, an inland lake with no outlet. The Dead Sea forms a boundary between Israel and Jordan. The surface of the Dead Sea is 1290 feet below sea level, the lowest place on the earth's surface; the water in some parts of the sea is over 1000 feet deep. Because of its extremely rapid rate of evaporation, the Dead Sea is very salty.

Other smaller gashes approach the Great Rift from the

eastern desert. These gashes are dry riverbeds, known as *wadis*. In the rainy months of January and February, the wadis can turn into rivers. This is very dangerous for travelers caught in a wadi during a downpour.

The Euphrates is one of the largest rivers of the Middle East. It originates in Turkey and cuts diagonally across the northeast corner of Syria before passing into Iraq. In Syria, the land south of the Euphrates is now mainly desert, except for the oasis of Palmyra where springs of water support large groves of date palms.

The most fertile area in Syria is next to the Anti-Lebanon Mountains. Short rivers and springs irrigate a strip of land between the mountains and the desert. Here are the cities of Damascus, Hama, Homs, and Aleppo.

Damascus is an ancient city; according to tradition, it was the home of Adam, Noah, and Abraham. Before it became part of the Roman Empire, Damascus was already practicing successful conservation of its water resources. Through the city winds the Barada River, which for centuries has fed water into canals that irrigate gardens and orchards.

Hama is another ancient city, situated in a deep river canyon. The Orontes River flows from Lebanon northward through the valley, turning huge water wheels called *noria*. These wooden wheels have been scooping irrigation water out of the Orontes for hundreds of years. As the current turns them, their wooden cups lift the water to aqueducts that carry it to orchards and houses.

In the plateau region of Turkey, there are rivers and streams that supply water to the area. Turkey also has excellent harbors and the magnificent city of Istanbul. This ancient metropolis has been a center of commerce, government, and culture for centuries, largely because of its location on the Bosporus, the waterway that separates Europe from Asia.

WATER IN THE ARABIAN PENINSULA

The Arabian Peninsula is dominated by Saudi Arabia. There are almost no lakes or permanent streams here, and some areas go without rainfall for years. One of the largest deserts in the world, the Rub al-Khali or "Empty Quarter," covers much of the southeastern section of the peninsula. Springs are few in the desert; wherever they appear, they support the patches of green known as oases. In the extreme southwest of Saudi Arabia is a fairly fertile strip of coastal mountain; there is enough rainfall here so that the valley sides can be farmed. Elsewhere, the land can be farmed only around deeply drilled wells or scattered oases.

In the heart of the peninsula is a vast plateau. Here is the Saudi capital of Riyadh, which means "gardens" in Arabic. Local springs and wells give this city much greenery.

The eastern section of the peninsula has a number of oases. It also has some of the most important fields, not of water but of that other valuable liquid resource, oil.

WATER SCARCITY AND DAILY LIFE

The magnificent river valleys make up only a small part of the entire Middle East. For example, the Nile directly affects only about five percent (one-twentieth) of Egypt's land. The remainder of the Middle East is a mixture of mountains, deserts, and plateaus. On the borders are large bodies of water, such as the Mediterranean Sea, the Caspian Sea, the Black Sea, the Red Sea, and the Gulf. Unlike the heavily populated river valleys, large areas of the Middle East receive little water. This scarcity of water has greatly influenced the way people live.

In villages and rural settlements, the most important decisions often involve the water supply. Some decisions, such as the distribution of water to the right fields at the right times, are made according to old traditions. In many larger settlements, a local official has the job of supervising water distribution. The water distributor knows when each owner needs water and where it can be gotten. He may pay out money for repairs and settle arguments about water rights.

Another important government official is the irrigation engineer stationed near each large canal. He decides when to open and close the floodgates that channel water from the main river to the villages and surrounding farmlands.

Where the water supply is plentiful and dependable, farmers are closely tied to their own plots of land. But in the mountain valleys of the Middle East, the fortunes of each village rise and fall according to the winter rains and the condition of the qanat or other irrigation system. Mountain peasants migrate from place to place, maintaining a balance between population and water supply.

In many parts of the world, water is an almost free resource that needs only to be transported. In Saudi Arabia and many other Middle Eastern countries, water is the most precious commodity. Agriculture must have water. Industry requires large amounts of it. And water is vital to the daily lives of the people.

Oil in the Middle East

In 1859, drillers struck oil near Titusville, Pennsylvania. From this first successful commercial oil well sprang the modern petroleum industry.

Today, the United States is the greatest consumer of petroleum (oil) products. But because its own supplies of oil are diminishing, the United States must depend upon oil imported from overseas, especially from the Middle East.

THE HISTORY OF OIL

The oil that comes from the earth in its crude form is commonly called petroleum. The story of petroleum began more than 500 million years ago when water covered much of what is now dry land. Geologists believe that billions of tiny animals and plants lived in these waters. As they died, their remains settled on the ancient sea floor and were buried in the sand and silt. Millions of years ago, as the seas dried up, these remains were subjected to great heat created by the pressure of the sediment gathering above them. They gradually were transformed into compounds of carbon and hydrogen, the oil and gas known as petroleum.

15

The word "petroleum" comes from the Greek words meaning "rock oil."

The gas found with crude oil in underground formations is natural gas. When it is found mixed with oil in the same underground reservoir, it is called "associated" or "solution" gas. (The Middle East also has fields of "non-associated" gas, found in reservoirs where no oil is present.)

As petroleum was being formed, the earth's movements trapped it in certain types of rock formations, creating pools or reservoirs of oil and gas. Since oil and gas are lighter than water, they rose upward through the water and through cracks in the rock until they reached rock that was too dense to pass through. They filled the upper parts of the traps, while the heavier water remained in the lower areas.

In the Middle East, early peoples were familiar with oil and gas that seeped up to the earth's surface through porous rock. The ancient Persians worshipped around burning oil seeps or natural gas leaks. The Judaic and Babylonian stories of the Great Flood state that asphalt or pitch (a form of petroleum) was used to caulk Noah's Ark and the vessel that saved the mythical Mesopotamian hero, Utnapishtim. Pitch was also used in ancient Egypt for mummification and to grease the axles of the pharaohs' chariots. The Greeks recorded how they destroyed an enemy fleet by pouring oil on the waters and setting it afire. And the Greek historian Herodotus wrote that petroleum pitch was used to caulk the walls of the Hanging Gardens of Babylon, one of the Seven Wonders of the World.

For thousands of years, surface leaks or tar pits were the only sources of petroleum. This casual use of petroleum changed dramatically when men developed drilling techniques, probed underground for oil pools, and struck oil in the United States and elsewhere during the second half of the nineteenth century.

Demand for petroleum increased rapidly as new uses for it were discovered.

THE SEARCH FOR OIL

As the search for oil went on, more and more attention was given to the Middle East, especially to Iran and to the Arabian Peninsula. And no wonder, for the wells of the Middle East are among the most productive in the world. We now know that the great Saudi Arabian oil deposits under the desert of the eastern province and its offshore waters make up approximately twenty-five percent (one-fourth) of the world's known reserves.

It is difficult to imagine that ancient seas and grassland once covered much of eastern Saudi Arabia. As the waters receded over millions of years, the sediments in many areas were pushed into anticlines (arch-like upward folds in the earth's layers) or domes; here, deposits of oil and gas were trapped in the sandstone and limestone under high pressure. Today eastern Saudi Arabia is a vast area of salt flats, gravel plains, and deserts. In some regions there has been no rain for a decade.

Rising above the plains between the coastal town of Dammam and the neighboring town of Dhahran are small hills that attracted the petroleum geologists who first saw them in 1933. These geologists were looking for anticlines and domes. They were certain that the hilly area they named the Dammam Dome would yield oil. And it did. For here is located the huge Ghawar oil field, over 150 miles long and 20 miles wide at one point. This giant has been yielding about five million barrels of crude oil daily. (In the oil industry, a barrel is a unit of measure equal to 42 gallons.)

This is only one example of the search for oil. Usually the process of finding oil and extracting it from the earth is more

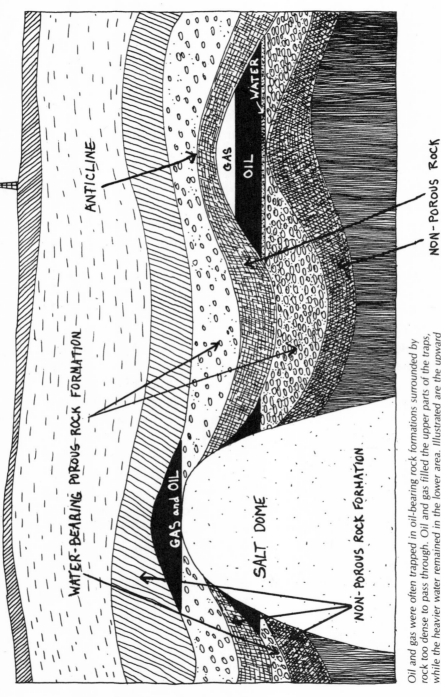

ANTICLINE

GAS

OIL

WATER

WATER-BEARING POROUS-ROCK FORMATION

GAS and OIL

SALT DOME

NON-POROUS ROCK FORMATION

NON-POROUS ROCK FORMATION

NON-POROUS ROCK

Oil and gas were often trapped in oil-bearing rock formations surrounded by rock too dense to pass through. Oil and gas filled the upper parts of the traps, while the heavier water remained in the lower area. Illustrated are the upward fold known as an anticline and a dome that resulted from the upward push of a large mass of salt. Here, deposits of oil and gas were trapped in the sandstone and limestone.

complicated. Oil may lie thousands of feet under deserts, mountains, marshes, or seas. Geologists cannot see through rock. But they do have tools to help them find out what kinds and shapes of rock lie beneath the surface.

First the searchers choose a particular area and study what is known about its rock formations. Then they obtain more detailed information with special instruments. These can measure variations in the earth's magnetic field and minute differences in the pull of gravity at the earth's surface. Such information tells geologists about the layers of rock that lie below.

In Saudi Arabia, the oil industry uses the technique of seismic exploration. (The word "seismic" refers to vibrations of the earth.) One method is to set off an explosive in a shallow hole; another technique is to use truck-mounted vibrating pads that actually shake the earth. The shock waves sent below ground are reflected off rock formations and bounced back to the surface. Aboard a seismic ship, vibratory devices like an air gun send out pulses to underwater rock formations. Detectors pick up and record the impulses. The scientists study the seismic results and learn the general characteristics of the underground structure. This helps them decide whether there is oil under the earth.

Satellite photography has become an important tool in the search for new energy supplies. One type of satellite orbits the earth, making a continuous set of images that yield clues to unexplored basins. This vehicle records not only visible light but also reflected infrared radiation as a series of scan lines which are placed side by side to form the image (similar to the way an image is formed on a television screen). Scientists project different colors through the film so that different features of the land will take on different colors. By varying the combinations of color lines, scientists can identify the geological features they are looking for.

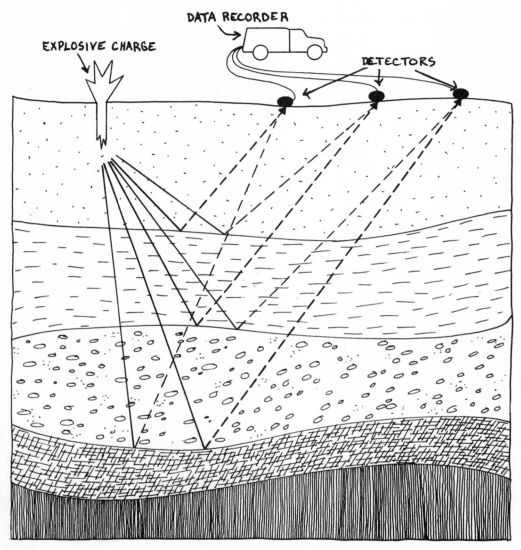

EXPLOSIVE CHARGE

DATA RECORDER

DETECTORS

Seismic Exploration. The explosion sets off shock waves that are reflected off underground rock formations and bounced back to detectors at the surface. The impulses are recorded and studied for information about the depth and types of underground rock formations.

SHOCK WAVES

REFLECTED WAVES

OIL FROM THE GROUND

After a site has been chosen, the drillers erect a derrick and attach a rotary drilling bit to a length of pipe. Most drilling rigs now use a "jackknife" derrick, a portable hinged unit that can be raised and lowered as one piece. The oil industry in the Middle East still uses standard derricks for special situations. These may be mobile steel structures set on big rollers or skids, or they may be dismantled piece by piece at one site and put together at the next one. Drilling in offshore waters requires different techniques. A fixed platform can be constructed over the site, or a mobile platform can be floated to the area and then anchored to the sea bottom.

In the middle of the derrick floor is a round steel rotary table with a hole in the center into which fits a heavy square pipe commonly known as a kelly. A bit is fastened to the lower end of a string of pipe, called "drill pipe." The round drill pipe is connected to the kelly. Engines turn the table and the bit is spun into the earth. As the drill goes deeper, more pipe lengths ("strings") are added.

Water is very important to the drilling operation. Throughout the procedure, "drilling mud"—a mixture of water, clay, and special chemicals—is pumped down through the hollow kelly and drill pipe, and circulated through the drill hole. When it reaches the bottom, the mud is forced out through openings in the bit. It returns to the surface outside the drill pipe. The mud carries chips of rock to the surface; these tell the drillers which geologic formations have been entered. The weight of the mud also controls the pressure of any oil, water, or gas that may be encountered by the drill bit.

As the hole is put down and oil is found, casings are installed in the well. Then, when the well is completed and oil is

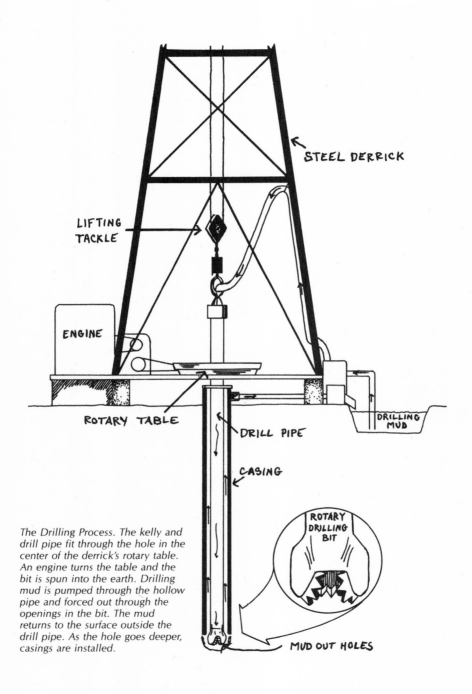

STEEL DERRICK

LIFTING TACKLE

ENGINE

ROTARY TABLE

DRILL PIPE

CASING

DRILLING MUD

ROTARY DRILLING BIT

MUD OUT HOLES

The Drilling Process. The kelly and drill pipe fit through the hole in the center of the derrick's rotary table. An engine turns the table and the bit is spun into the earth. Drilling mud is pumped through the hollow pipe and forced out through the openings in the bit. The mud returns to the surface outside the drill pipe. As the hole goes deeper, casings are installed.

flowing, the derrick, drilling platform, tools, and crew move on to another test site. All that remains is a system of valves, meters, and pipes called a Christmas tree because of its many branchlike fittings. This "tree" controls the flow of natural gas and oil from the moment the well begins to produce.

OIL PRESSURE

One of the features of oil in the Arabian Peninsula is that it flows to the surface under its own great natural pressure. This pressure comes primarily from the dissolved gas trapped with the crude oil in the underground oil-bearing reservoir. When the oil drill opens the reservoir, the dissolved gas is allowed to expand. This expansion forces the oil-gas mixture to flow to the surface. Water lying beneath the oil in the reservoir displaces the oil as it is removed.

As the oil-gas mixture rises up the well bore, the gas bubbles begin to act like bubbles in a bottle of soda or carbonated beverage. The gas starts to separate out of the oil. Above ground, the natural pressure is still enough to push the oil and gas through pipes to plants where the gas and oil are separated.

At the oil well, meanwhile, the pressure has been decreasing underground as the gas-oil mixture escapes. Over a period of time, the oil field's natural pressure is reduced and must be assisted. This is usually done by injecting either water or gas into the reservoir.

Water now becomes critically important to the operation of the oil field. In the huge fields of eastern Saudi Arabia, for example, engineers inject millions of barrels of non-drinkable water every day to maintain pressure. The water moves in behind the oil and gas and helps to push the oil ahead of it to the wells that are operating.

The sources of water are often near the oilfields—in aquifers, which are layers of rock and sand containing water, located several hundred feet below ground. Also used is seawater pumped from the Gulf and treated before it is injected into the water-bearing area around the oil reservoir.

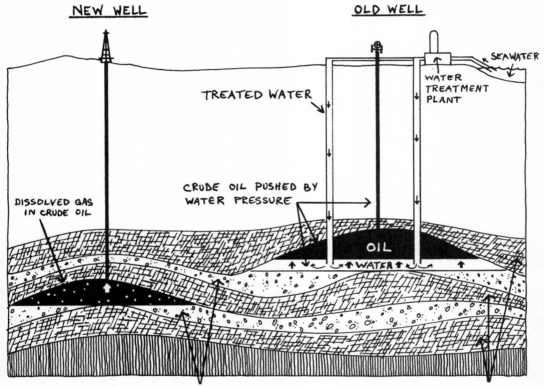

NEW WELL

OLD WELL

TREATED WATER

SEAWATER

WATER TREATMENT PLANT

CRUDE OIL PUSHED BY WATER PRESSURE

DISSOLVED GAS IN CRUDE OIL

OIL

WATER

WATER-BEARING ROCK FORMATIONS

NON-POROUS ROCK FORMATIONS

New Well Pumping Crude Oil Containing Dissolved Gas. When the drill opens the oil reservoir, dissolved gas is allowed to expand. This expansion forces the oil-gas mixture to flow to the surface.

Old Well. The natural pressure must be assisted. Here, seawater is treated and injected into the water-bearing area around the oil. The water moves in behind the oil and associated gas and helps to push them ahead of it to the operating well.

FROM WELL TO REFINERY

Once the mixture of crude oil and natural gas is above ground at the well, it must be processed and transported to refineries and storage tanks. The crude oil flows from the Christmas tree at the wellhead to a gas-oil separator plant (GOSP). Inside the GOSP, the gas, being lighter, moves to the top of the vessel while the heavier oil collects at the bottom. Increasing use is being made of this associated gas, which is piped to gas plants for processing into gas products for local industrial use and for export.

The crude oil from many GOSPS is sour crude; that is, it contains hydrogen sulfide. Hydrogen sulfide, as a gas, is poisonous; when dissolved in water, it forms a corrosive acid. To transport sour crude in tankers is undesirable. Therefore, it must be "sweetened" by a process called stabilization. The crude oil flows from the GOSP to a stabilizer where hydrogen sulfide and other impurities are removed. After stabilization, the crude oil is pumped to tank farms, to an exporting pipeline, or to other distribution centers.

The entire oil production process involves much work and planning for proper transportation and storage. Pipelines, barges, highway tank trucks, seagoing tankers, and railroad tank cars are used to move the crude oil and petroleum products. Storage tanks dot the land; some of them can hold more than one million barrels of oil. Most petroleum products or crude oil go to storage tanks to await transfer to tankers or barges for the remaining journey to world markets. Smaller quantities of crude oil may be exported by pipeline.

While some pipelines are rather short because the producing wells are near water terminals (as in eastern Saudi Arabia and southwestern Iran), other pipelines stretch for hundreds of miles. For many years the pipeline known as Tapline (short for Trans-Arabian Pipe Line) transported crude oil from the eastern

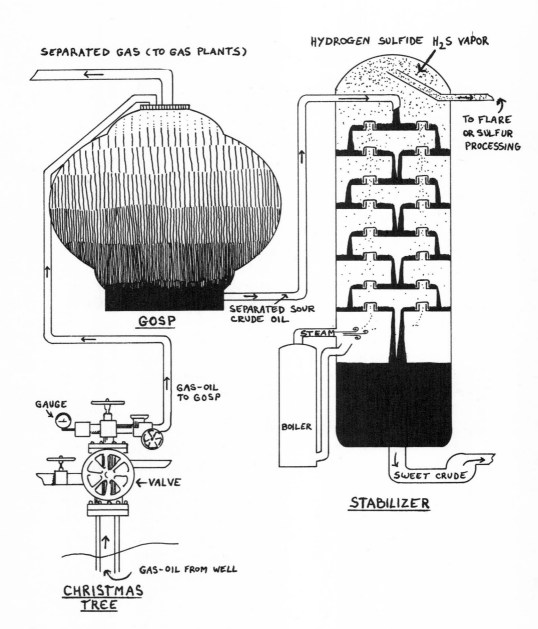

SEPARATED GAS (TO GAS PLANTS)

HYDROGEN SULFIDE H₂S VAPOR

TO FLARE OR SULFUR PROCESSING

GOSP

SEPARATED SOUR CRUDE OIL

STEAM

BOILER

SWEET CRUDE

STABILIZER

GAS-OIL TO GOSP

GAUGE

←VALVE

↑ GAS-OIL FROM WELL

CHRISTMAS TREE

The Path of Oil from the Christmas Tree to the Stabilizer. The crude oil flows from the Christmas tree to a gas-oil separator plant (GOSP), and then to a stabilizer to remove the hydrogen sulfide. From the stabilizer the crude is pumped to storage tanks or to distribution centers.

part of the Arabian Peninsula to the Lebanese port of Sidon on the Mediterranean. Pipelines in the interior of Iraq carry oil to other ports on the Mediterranean and to ports on the Gulf.

Some Middle Eastern pipelines are so large that you could probably walk inside them. To make sure the pipes are covered well enough for safe operation, they are usually laid in deep ditches. After the line is constructed, an operator controls the pumping pressure and the rate of flow. Some types of oil are heavy and slow-moving, while others are lighter and move much faster through the pipe.

Much of the oil carried in pipelines ends at a refinery. The Abadan refinery in southwestern Iran is one of the largest in the world. Another gigantic refinery is at Ras Tanura, in Saudi Arabia.

OIL INTO GASOLINE

At the refinery, crude oil is heated and separated into different products. Crude oil is a mixture of thousands of different hydrocarbons (compounds of carbon and hydrogen). Each oil field has its own mixture, and the mixtures vary widely from one field to the next. The assortment of hydrocarbons in the crude oil and the way in which they are combined determine the particular type and character of the crude oil. Crude oils therefore do not all look alike. They may be of different colors—brown, black, green, amber, or almost colorless.

Each type of crude oil requires a different kind of handling and processing. Four standard grades are Arabian Heavy, Arabian Medium, Arabian Light, and Arabian Extra Light. The most important grade is Arabian Light crude; many oil-producing countries use the price for this grade as the standard to which prices for other crudes are related.

Crude oil contains ingredients other than hydrocarbons. A

favorite type on the world market is known as "sweet" (with certain types being called "Saudi sweet"). This crude oil has a sulfur content of less than one percent, and is therefore considered "sweet." Crude oils containing more than one percent of sulfur are usually called "sour crude."

In the refining process, the basic hydrogen-carbon structure of the crude oil is rearranged. When it is heated, crude oil becomes vaporous. The vapors of so-called heavier hydrocarbons condense at one level in a column called a "fractionating column." The vapors of lighter hydrocarbons condense at other levels. In this process of distillation or fractionating at various levels, gasoline is separated at the top, then kerosene below, followed by fuel oils, lubricating oils, and other products. The main product left over at the bottom is asphalt. Those gases that do not change from a gas to a liquid are drawn off at the top of the column.

Again we see the importance of water for oil. The refinery needs large quantities of purified water for cooling and processing. Without this water, the refinery could not operate efficiently.

OIL TRANSPORT

Whether it is refined or kept as simple crude oil, the oil now takes another step along the way. This time, the key element is the modern seagoing tanker.

Tankers are divided into compartments for carrying liquid cargoes. The biggest tankers, called Very Large Crude Carriers (VLCCs), can transport several million barrels of oil on a single voyage. These huge ships, however, can move only in deep waters. In the Middle East oil trade, many tankers must pass through narrow stretches of water, such as the Strait of Hormuz, which is the narrow opening of the Gulf. VLCCs manage to pass

FRACTIONATING COLUMN

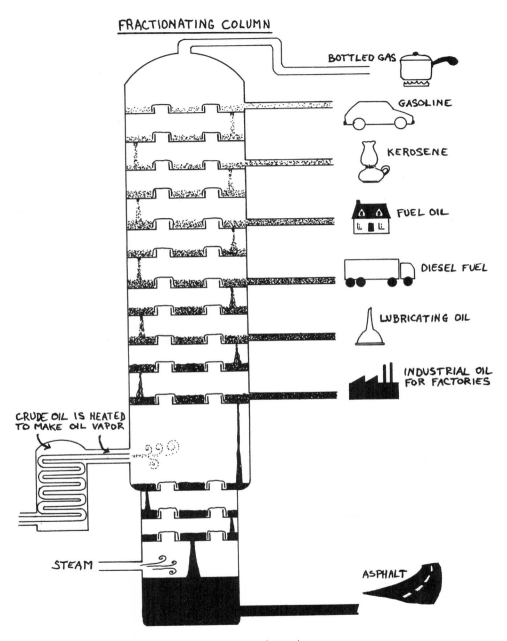

BOTTLED GAS

GASOLINE

KEROSENE

FUEL OIL

DIESEL FUEL

LUBRICATING OIL

INDUSTRIAL OIL FOR FACTORIES

CRUDE OIL IS HEATED TO MAKE OIL VAPOR

STEAM

ASPHALT

In the fractionating column, oil vapors rise, grow cooler, and condense. They then separate out at various levels, heaviest toward the bottom, lightest at the top. Those gases that do not change from a gas to a liquid are drawn off at the top of the column.

through the Strait, but they cannot use another popular transit route, the Suez Canal, when they are fully loaded.

Many countries, including the United States, are concerned about the free movement of oil tankers. These nations would suffer if shipments were blocked at a strategic point like the Strait of Hormuz or the Suez Canal. So they welcome having a choice of tanker or pipeline.

For example, much of the Middle Eastern oil comes from fields in the eastern part of the Arabian Peninsula, especially the Ghawar field in Saudi Arabia. Normally, this oil moves in tankers that load the oil at ports in the Gulf, then pass through the Strait of Hormuz, and onward to their destinations overseas. To provide itself with an alternative export terminal and to service refineries on the west coast, Saudi Arabia is building a huge pipeline that links the Ghawar oil field to Yanbu, a port on the Red Sea 750 miles away. The completed project will enable Saudi Arabia to move almost two million barrels of crude oil daily, with a transportation savings of some 2100 miles for oil routed to the Mediterranean Sea.

With the shipment of oil by tanker or pipeline, the countries of the Middle East have completed the production process. They can now enjoy the large amounts of money they receive from oil sales to other nations.

Oil and Water in Today's Middle East

The money that comes from oil operations has had a dramatic impact on the Middle East. It has allowed many governments to set up intensive development programs for their countries. Among the smaller nations of the region, Qatar, Kuwait, and the United Arab Emirates especially have invested large amounts of money in national improvement projects.

But in many Middle Eastern countries, the new-found wealth from oil has presented problems. Traditional ways of life have been changed or questioned. Because the oil countries of the Middle East do not have enough trained people to manage the new wealth and the programs it pays for, they have had to open their borders to millions of foreign workers, managers, and consultants.

To meet the world's increasing energy requirements, Middle Eastern oil producers realize that they must use their oil resources and income wisely. They have become more and more careful to safeguard their own interests. In the early 1960's, the governments of Saudi Arabia, Iran, Iraq, and Kuwait joined with the South American government of Venezuela to set up the Organization of Petroleum Exporting Countries (OPEC). Since then, OPEC has expanded its membership to include countries from Africa and Asia, and has greatly increased its influence in the world's oil affairs. In addition, Arab countries of the Middle East established the Organization of Arab Petroleum Exporting Countries (OAPEC).

Many Middle Easterners wonder about the future of oil in their ground. When this valuable natural resource is used up, income will disappear. This partly explains why so many oil-rich countries in the Middle East are reluctant to have their oil pumped out of the ground as rapidly as possible. They would rather control the flow of oil so that this treasure will remain available for many years.

Of all the Middle Eastern countries, the kingdom of Saudi Arabia is one that has done the most to manage its oil reserves. In just a few years it has become a very important participant in world affairs. It probably has gone the furthest in its development programs, based on oil income, for industry, health, education, housing, and agriculture.

But to build a modern state in the Middle East, more than oil is required. There still remains the problem of water. Industry and agriculture especially are putting increasing demands on the area's water reserves.

Underlying all modernization programs in most of the Middle East is the fact that water is scarce. And in any attempt to build a modern economy, water poverty can seriously offset oil wealth.

WATER TECHNOLOGY IN THE MIDDLE EAST

There are two ways to increase a water supply: to find new sources of usable water, and to improve management of the water supply so that the right amount is available at the right time.

New supplies of water can be created by collecting and transporting runoff rainwater. Runoff agriculture was developed thousands of years ago by farmers in the Middle East. They cleared hillsides to increase the amount of runoff water, and they built walls and ditches to collect the water and make it run down to lower-lying fields.

Many of these ancient systems were neglected over the years, but the basic idea would still work today. The oil-producing countries of the Middle East could use their heavy petroleum product, asphalt, to seal the soil and construct water-harvesting basins. Once the runoff rainwater has been collected, it can be used for agricultural needs.

A permanent problem facing irrigated agriculture in the Middle East is the accumulation of salt in the soil. However, it has been shown that in parts of the Middle East, saline ground-water (water from the earth) can be brought into the irrigation system, especially for highly tolerant crops such as cotton, barley, and wheat. (Untreated seawater is unsuitable because its salt content is about ten times the amount that even these crops can tolerate.) The method used is trickle or drip irrigation, which feeds small but continuous amounts of water directly to the plant roots without spraying from above. The salinity of the soil is kept to a minimum under this method.

Large reserves of water are available underground in aquifers. These are water-bearing formations of sandstone or limestone. Aquifers under Middle Eastern deserts, such as those in Saudi Arabia and western Egypt, contain trapped "fossil" water that is over ten thousand years old. But fossil aquifers must be carefully farmed. Otherwise, they may suddenly empty or become salinated by other underground water. If efficiently tapped, the aquifers of the Middle East could yield hundreds of millions of gallons of fresh water daily.

But aquifer water, like oil, is limited in quantity. Middle East nations therefore may prefer to reserve the aquifer water supply and to turn, instead, to the desalting of seawater.

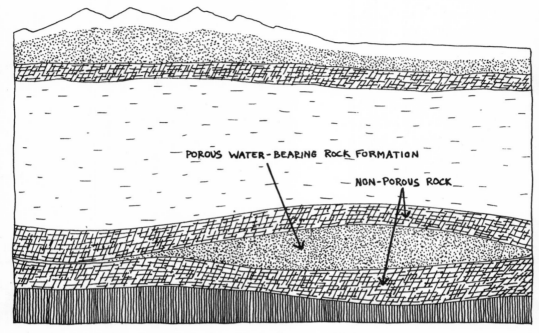

A "fossil" aquifer contains trapped water that is thousands of years old. This deep aquifer may be a water-bearing formation of sandstone or limestone. Like oil, fossil aquifer water is not replaceable and therefore is limited in quantity.

Saudi Arabia and other countries in the Arabian Peninsula have one ready source of water—the seawater of the Gulf and the Red Sea. Seawater has not been used for farming because the salts in it stunt the plants' growth and reduce the yield of crops.

Many engineers, however, believe that seawater will be the major source of water for many Arab countries. Groundwater, where it is available, will supplement the seawater. Modern technology has made it possible to desalinate (remove the salt from) huge quantities of seawater at a cost that the now-rich oil countries can afford. Billions of dollars will probably be spent on water distribution systems and desalination plants during the next several years.

People have also thought about some extraordinary methods to obtain water for the Middle East. Since most of the world's fresh water is trapped in polar ice, why not move an iceberg from the Antarctic to the Middle East? But just as there are questions about water rights on rivers like the Nile, there are possible legal and political problems about moving icebergs in international shipping lanes. Another question is how to get the ice to melt properly once it arrives in the Middle East.

The countries of the Middle East know that they must work on their problems of water supply. They need to find their natural water resources, to use remote sensing techniques, to reclaim or recycle water. They want to build more water supply systems, to drill and repair and replace wells, to construct dams, and to improve the quality of their drinking water.

Fortunately, the substantial income from oil production now permits hope for the future of the Middle East. Saudi Arabia, for example, has undertaken a multi-billion dollar water development program that includes new water pipelines and desalination plants, as well as searches for deep underground water sources thousands of years old.

Before the year 2000, the image of the Middle East as a vast, waterless area could easily change, thanks to that other precious liquid—oil.

The Uses of Petroleum

Thousands of products we use every day are made partly or entirely from petroleum:

Insecticides	Batteries	Detergents for cleaning
Polishes	Antifreeze	Food preservatives
Shoes	Perfumes	Wash-and-wear fabrics
Paints	Explosives	Ointments and creams
Fertilizers	Varnishes	Photographic film
Plastics	Matches	Long-playing records
Tires	Lipstick	Pharmaceuticals
Aspirin	Adhesives	Rubbing alcohol
Vitamins	Candles	Cleaning compounds
Ink	Resins	Solvents for paint
Dyes	Road oil	Synthetic fiber
Hand lotion	Asphalt	Waxed paper
Nose drops	Grease	Nylon stockings
Soaps	Chewing gum	Lubricating oil
Roofing	Flooring	Synthetic rubber
Crayons	Weed killer	

We also use forms of petroleum for our energy needs:

Gasoline for cars and trucks
Diesel fuel for cars, trucks, trains, and ships
Liquid petroleum gas for heating, cooking, and
   refrigerating
Aviation gasoline and jet fuel for air transportation
Kerosene for heat, lighting, and insecticide
Natural gas and fuel oil for home heating
Bunker fuel for ships
Gas for cooking, metal cutting, and lighting
Industrial fuel oil for industry and plants

Glossary

anticline   an arch-like upward fold of rock layers in the earth, in which the layers bend downward in opposite directions from the crest (top); this fold may form a trap for oil and gas.

aqueduct   a conduit or channel through which water is carried.

aquifer   a formation of rock and sand, such as sandstone or limestone, that holds water trapped underground; "fossil" aquifers are deep formations containing old water which is not replaceable.

barrel   in the oil industry, a unit of measure equal to 42 gallons.

casing   a tube or pipe used as a lining in a well.

caulk   to make seams (of a boat) watertight by filling with a waterproofing material.

crude oil   liquid form of petroleum as it comes out of the ground; it is a mixture of hydrocarbons and other ingredients.

dam   a barrier to prevent the flow of water; a barrier built on a watercourse (river) for holding water for storage.

desalination   the process of removing unwanted, dissolved mineral salts from saline water.

dome   a natural underground formation resembling an upside-down bowl, often resulting from the upward push of a large mass of salt; oil and natural gas may be found adjacent to or on top of the dome.

evaporation the changing of a fluid (water) into vapor or invisible minute particles.

fractionation (distillation) the separation of crude oil and natural gas into parts. Oil, when heated, turns to vapor; the vapors rise, grow cooler, and condense in the fractionating tower; they then separate out at various levels, the heaviest toward the bottom, the lightest at the top; the oil that did not turn to vapor remains at the bottom.

fresh water natural water without salt.

galleries underground corridors or passageways used for collecting water in a qanat.

gas a substance (like air) that has no definite shape or volume (in contrast to a liquid or solid).

geologist one who studies the history of the earth and its solid matter; a rock expert.

groundwater water from the earth that supplies springs and wells.

hydrocarbon a chemical compound of hydrogen and carbon (*see* petroleum).

impact forceful effect.

inject to drive or force a substance into another substance.

irrigation supplying with water by artificial means.

natural gas a form of petroleum found in underground formations either with crude oil or by itself; a gas consisting of methane and other hydrocarbons.

oasis (*plural:* oases) in an arid region, a fertile or green area watered by natural springs and man-made wells.

oil a burnable (combustible) type of liquid that is not soluble in water; the name often given to crude oil, a form of petroleum (*see* crude oil).

oil reserves the amount of crude oil available in the ground; "proved reserves" refers to reserves that have actually been discovered.

oil well a well from which crude oil and associated gas are obtained.

petroleum a mixture of hydrocarbons (hydrogen and carbon) found underground. Petroleum has three basic forms: solid (asphalt), liquid (crude oil), and gas (natural gas); it is prepared for use as gasoline or other products.

pipeline a pipe transportation system for moving gas and oil.

refinery a plant where crude oil is heated and separated into different products.

refining the manufacture of crude oils into petroleum products by separating crude oils into major parts and converting (changing) these parts into finished products.

reservoir for oil an underground formation of porous rock holding droplets of gas and oil; this formation is surrounded by nonporous rock which creates a "reservoir" in which the gas and oil are trapped.

runoff water from snow or rain that runs or flows over the earth's surface.

saline, salinity containing or consisting of salt. Soil salinity can be caused by aboveground saline waters or by saline water below the ground that rises to the surface; salinity is measured by the amount of dissolved solids in the substance.

sediment matter that settles to the bottom of a liquid.

seismic relating to the vibration or shaking of the earth, such as a shockwave sent below ground and caused by an explosion or by a vibrator.

silt a deposit (by a river) of loose sedimentary material containing very small pieces of rock.

sluice an artificial water passage fitted with a gate or valve for regulating or stopping flow.

stabilization the process of removing unwanted gases and impurities from crude oil.

tolerate (salt) to endure or resist the action of salt without serious injury.

vapor   a substance in the gaseous state.

wadi   the valley or bed of a stream, in the Middle East, that is usually dry except during the rainy season.

water table   the level or upper limit of that section of ground completely saturated (filled) with water.

water terminal (marine terminal)   construction by a body of water that is especially designed for the storage of crude oil, gas, and refined products, and for their transfer from pipeline or storage unit to tankers or barges.

Index

rift, 11
Riyadh, 13
rock formation, 16, 19
Roman Empire, 12
rotary table, 21
Rub al-Khali, 13
runoff agriculture, 32
runoff rainwater, 32
rural settlements, 13

salinity, 6, 7, 8, 11, 33
salt accumulation, 7, 33
sand, 15, 24
sandstone, 17, 33
satellite photography, 19
Saudi Arabia, 13, 14, 17, 19, 23, 25,
    27, 30, 31, 33, 34, 35
scientists, 19
seawater, 33, 34
sediment, 15, 17
seismic exploration, 19
settled areas, 8
Shatt Al-Arab region, 8
Shatt Al-Arab River, 8
shock waves, 19
Sidon, 27
silt, 4, 7, 15
South America, 31
Soviet Union, 11
stabilization, 25
storage tanks, 25
Strait of Hormuz, 28, 30
Sudan, 6, 7
Sudd, 6
Suez Canal, 30
sulfur, 28
surface leaks, 16
"sweet," "sweetening," 25, 28
Syria, 12

tank farms, 25
Tapline, 25
terminals, water (marine), 25

Tigris River, 4, 7, 8
Titusville, PA, 15
traditions, 14, 31
Trans-Arabian Pipe Line, see Tapline
trickle irrigation, 33
Turkey, 8, 11, 12

Uganda, 6
underground reservoir, 8, 10, 16, 23
United Arab Emirates, 31
United States, 1, 15, 16, 30

vapor, 28
Venezuela, 31
VLCC (Very Large Crude Carrier), 28,
    30

wadi, 12
water
    development programs, 25
    distribution systems, 14, 35
    fresh, 11, 33, 35
    harvesting basins, 33
    injection, 23, 24
    management and control, 6, 7, 32
    needs for, 1
    resources, 1, 7, 11, 12, 14, 35
    rights, 8, 14, 35
    saline, 6
    scarcity, 13, 32
    sources, 6, 24, 32, 34, 35
    supplies, 1, 6, 7, 13, 14, 32, 35
    surplus, 7
    technology, 32
    treatment, 24
    underground, 8, 10, 11, 33, 35
    waste, 7
water and political problems, 7, 8, 35
water-bearing formations, 33
water table, 10
water wheels, 6, 12

Yanbu, 30